NIGHTS IN SOLITUDE

THE SCENE OF UNIQUE THOUGHTS

AADIL GHULAM BHAT

AADIL GHULAM BHAT

Dedicated to the loving memory of my family, friends and teachers. without teachers, i wouldn't have come redunceacross an author in me. I am thankful to my friends, who encouraged me at every moment and support me in this successful journy. I am thankful to my parents who supported me in every aspect.

" Burmese in understanding and sympathy even in prudence.It was my deciet, that they are the colours of my love"

_______________AADIL GHULAM

BHAT_____________________

Contents

Contents

Contents

Preface

Thanks to Almighty, who made capable and gave me ability to collect my emotions and express them into words.it is indeed encouraging for me to know that there is great demand and scope of poetry in this era. I am grateful to my Lord that the time has finally reached , that i am in a position to introduce my newly arriving entitled-" NIGHTS IN SOLITUDE" for all readers across the globe especially poetry readers..

Poetry is one of the most prestigous forms of writing. It is verse based writing with ocean of feelings and emotions, beautify the thoughts in literature. Poetry is not what we read, poetry is what we observe, what we feel, what we suffer and how do we express real feelings. poetry starts from heart which include real emotions. poetry is hope, postivity, experience, love, affection etc. For poet it is a life, breath , heartbeat and everything.

The book is made ready for many heart touching poems about real feelings, bond of emotions and endurance.

As long as i understood the style,real meaning and scenario of poetry. I have also started my journey in the feild of poetry.i start writing to endure myself.

Aadil Ghulam Bhat

Hablishi, Kulgam

J & K India

Contact: +91 7889852115

Acknowledgements

Primarily i would thank Allah for being able to complete this book with success. Then i would like to thank Mr. Bhargava Adepally co-founder & CTO of NOTION PRESS PUBLISHING whose valuable guidance has been the ones that helped me pacth this book and make it full proof success, his suggestions and his instructions has served as the major contributor towards the completion of the book.

Last but not the least i would like to thank my friends who have helped me a lot .

Aadil Ghulam Bhat.

1. BLACK HOURS

Although i was immersed in the ocean of emotions.
Asserting oneself was to raise the voice of retention.
Solitairness, the secret of heart came to lips.
All over, mild nights seemed of right.
Alack, alack-a day, the silence of lips fell into heart.
I'm buried inside my soul, including my deadly thoughts.
Thou had grasp me in fingers of grief.
Giddily, it is enough to make angeles weep.
I zipped around, i'll be with you in two shakes.
The fear of drowning had quaked me in my boots.
How did i explain my painful odium.
Indeed, as a loveless life is a living death".

About Author: Aadil Ghulam Bhat is an author of two books, "100 YEARS OF MY PAINFUL NIGHTS" and "NIGHTS IN SOLITUDE".

Besides english poetry he also has a contribution in urdu poerty and novels too. Although Aadil Gulam associate his emotions with words that make poetry. He choose one of the many different ways to convey his message.

Aadil Ghulam Bhat has persued his bachalor's degree in non-medical at Govt.Degree College Anantnag (J&K). Being a non-medical student he used to write something in feild of literature. Due course of time apart from his accademic career he start to compose his poetry and finally end up his bit of emotions, feelings and thoughts in form of book.

The poem " BLACK HOURS" is written in escatsy manner and the style of writing is quite impressive over the entire collection of book.

2. A STATE OF BREATHLESS EXPECTANCY

The sweep of mind, i got shocked for a moment.

I'm shaken with anxiety, hallucination, my branches broke down.

Beneath the blue sky, upon the golden earth.

Thy dear steps, there'll surely a voice of dearth.

Beyond envious thoughts, i need a cordial courage.

I'm ere in the terrace, and crow is calling.

Thy door steps, i found the oceans of same depths i drowned.

I found yore, and lost the thing i never found.

I'm looking to skies, my hopes are rain.

It will finally come across my line, endure my pain.

About Author: Aadil Ghulam Bhat is an author of two books, "100 YEARS OF MY PAINFUL NIGHTS" and

"NIGHTS IN SOLITUDE".

Besides english poetry he also has a contribution in urdu poerty and novels too. Although Aadil Gulam associate his emotions with words that make poetry. He choose one of the many different ways to convey his message.

Aadil Ghulam Bhat has persued his bachalor's degree in non-medical at Govt.Degree College Anantnag (J&K). Being a non-medical student he used to write something in feild of literature. Due course of time apart from his accademic career he start to compose his poetry and finally end up his bit of emotions, feelings and thoughts in form of book.

The poem "A STSTE OF BREATHLESS EXPACTANCY" is written in escatsy manner and the style of writing is quite impressive over the entire collection of book.

3. I FEEL PAIN

Nights are cold, memories are eld.

In the lap of voice I was ere.

Was harking some voice in late night air.

I thought a Mead and sweet dream with perfervid.

I prefer lenity so calm, deep minded with ease.

I thought I was overwhelmed by its grace.

Slowly, gently I went to to appease.

Like a morning breeze blew on my face.

Her love gone quietly, patiently and stygain.

Didn't live, couldn't slumber. Didn't even endure pain.

I asked my mind if I had gone through the rain.

I felt hard pain. Again, again and again.

About Author: Aadil Ghulam Bhat is an author of two books, "100 YEARS OF MY PAINFUL NIGHTS" and "NIGHTS IN SOLITUDE".

Besides english poetry he also has a contribution in urdu poerty and novels too. Although Aadil Gulam associate his emotions with words that make poetry. He choose one of the many different ways to convey his message.

Aadil Ghulam Bhat has persued his bachalor's degree in non-medical at Govt.Degree College Anantnag (J&K). Being a non-medical student he used to write something in feild of literature. Due course of time apart from his accademic career he start to compose his poetry and finally end up his bit of emotions, feelings and thoughts in form of book.

The poem " I FEEL PAIN" is written in escatsy manner and the style of writing is quite impressive over the entire collection of book.

4. ELEGY

When i close my eyes and think of you .
Like a dream, i found myself in an avenue.
You don't know whether the soul is mine or pain.
You don't know what you are looking for again.
My world came to be a painful and shocking halt.
My heart is impriosned, feelings are grasp in vault.
I'm alone deep in pain, hogtied like a prisoner.
I've lost myself in a dingle. behold darkling i slumber.
CWhen i close my eyes and think of you.
I found myself in the corner of a blithe queue.

About Author: Aadil Ghulam Bhat is an author of two books, "100 YEARS OF MY PAINFUL NIGHTS" and "NIGHTS IN SOLITUDE".
Besides english poetry he also has a contribution in urdu poerty and novels too. Although Aadil Gulam associate his emotions with words that make poetry. He choose one of

the many different ways to convey his message.
Aadil Ghulam Bhat has persued his bachalor's degree in
non-medical at Govt.Degree College Anantnag (J&K).
Being a non-medical student he used to write something in
feild of literature. Due course of time apart from his
accademic career he start to compose his poetry and finally
end up his bit of emotions, feelings and thoughts in form of
book.
The poem " ELEGY" is written in escatsy manner and the
style of writing is quite impressive over the entire collection
of book.

5. DREAM IN WONDERLAND

Beheaded horse, running in the grip of fatigue
Chick shrieking, humming on the twig of a tree.
I'm afraid, my pale hands tremble with tremor.
In the lap of tree, like a child boy unwillingly to school.
Dicephaly snake, creeping around my frightened yard.
My look shifted to the strange man, with spectacles on nose.
Tall, white curly hair with informal beard cut.
With magical power, dragged me to other side.
The snake entered the hole, stood tail as message.
The stranger put his hand on my head and left me to sleep.

About Author: Aadil Ghulam Bhat is an author of two books, "100 YEARS OF MY PAINFUL NIGHTS" and "NIGHTS IN SOLITUDE".

Besides english poetry he also has a contribution in urdu poerty and novels too. Although Aadil Gulam associate his emotions with words that make poetry. He choose one of the many different ways to convey his message.

Aadil Ghulam Bhat has persued his bachalor's degree in non-medical at Govt.Degree College Anantnag (J&K). Being a non-medical student he used to write something in feild of literature. Due course of time apart from his accademic career he start to compose his poetry and finally end up his bit of emotions, feelings and thoughts in form of book.

The poem "DREAM IN WONDERLAND" is written in escatsy manner and the style of writing is quite impressive over the entire collection of book.

6. IN A STATE OF DECEIT

The sweep of mind, i got shocked for a moment.
I'm shaken with anxiety, hallucination, my branches broke down
Beneath the blue sky, upon the golden earth.
Thy dear steps, there'll surely a voice of dearth.
Beyond envious thoughts, i need a cordial courage.
I'm ere in the terrace, and crow is calling.
Thy door steps, i found the oceans of same depths i drowned.
I found yore, and lost the thing i never found.
I'm looking to skies, my hopes are rain.
It will finally come across my line, endure my pain.

About Author: Aadil Ghulam Bhat is an author of two books, "100 YEARS OF MY PAINFUL NIGHTS" and "NIGHTS IN SOLITUDE".

Besides english poetry he also has a contribution in urdu poerty and novels too. Although Aadil Gulam associate his emotions with words that make poetry. He choose one of the many different ways to convey his message.

Aadil Ghulam Bhat has persued his bachalor's degree in non-medical at Govt.Degree College Anantnag (J&K). Being a non-medical student he used to write something in feild of literature. Due course of time apart from his accademic career he start to compose his poetry and finally end up his bit of emotions, feelings and thoughts in form of book.

The poem "DREAM IN WONDERLAND" is written in escatsy manner and the style of writing is quite impressive over the entire collection of book.

7. A LOST BALL IN WEEDS

Look at the mystery of the streets, thoughts of isolation.
I'm buried in the courtyard of segregation.
Oh! The orange blush of heart-catching sun
What do i know of thou. I'm decorated with imitation.
Thy dear steps which were here yore__now in neck of woods.
Oh! You bound me in the distress, dreams were shattered.
It's been a blue moon, I'm still drowning in emotions.
Sitting on catrenary, a watched pot never boils.
As long as I'm waiting. I'm outside half, salt in my wounds.
I'm usually leaning towards lea, running down a lot of dolour.
Every moment i cried for a cruel sense in bad thoughts.
Even more hopes were wasted in the parts,fabricated not at all.

About Author: Aadil Ghulam Bhat is an author of two
books, "100 YEARS OF MY PAINFUL NIGHTS" and

"NIGHTS IN SOLITUDE".

Besides english poetry he also has a contribution in urdu poerty and novels too. Although Aadil Gulam associate his emotions with words that make poetry. He choose one of the many different ways to convey his message.

Aadil Ghulam Bhat has persued his bachalor's degree in non-medical at Govt.Degree College Anantnag (J&K). Being a non-medical student he used to write something in feild of literature. Due course of time apart from his accademic career he start to compose his poetry and finally end up his bit of emotions, feelings and thoughts in form of book.

The poem "A LOST BALL IN WEEDS" is written in escatsy manner and the style of writing is quite impressive over the entire collection of book.

8. THE AGE OF MIRACLES

All the things has a cause to happen.
The sun, the morning, the stars, the night,
The golden sun to morning, the stars to night.
Merely all played the age of miracles.
The creeping school boy, with utmost unwillingness.
The solider with oath at lips, adhere solidarity.
Then the beggars to congested streets, struggle to live.
They all played the age of miracles.
The birds return to their nests, with hope.
Some whining acts of patients, bearing the pain.
Enormous joy of prisoners, to be released
And these just played the ages of miracles.

About Author: Aadil Ghulam Bhat is an author of two books, "100 YEARS OF MY PAINFUL NIGHTS" and

"NIGHTS IN SOLITUDE".

Besides english poetry he also has a contribution in urdu poerty and novels too. Although Aadil Gulam associate his emotions with words that make poetry. He choose one of the many different ways to convey his message.

Aadil Ghulam Bhat has persued his bachalor's degree in non-medical at Govt.Degree College Anantnag (J&K). Being a non-medical student he used to write something in feild of literature. Due course of time apart from his accademic career he start to compose his poetry and finally end up his bit of emotions, feelings and thoughts in form of book.

The poem "THE AGE OF MIRACLES" is written in escatsy manner and the style of writing is quite impressive over the entire collection of book.

9. ONCE AGAIN ELD MEMORIES REGAIN

To come to their streets, I have left this quirk.

In her memories, I was demerged into depths.

I was roaming in crowded streets, waiting for you to come.

Although! I was shaken, I used to take care of you as well.

Your shadow also meant for me, I was lost in thee.

The distance is in flame, __ain't find anything to me.

I used to get off odds and ends.

Many were of same stripe, I was of two minds.

Oh, How will I fall sleep, so patiently, pale rider.

In your eld, hidden memories__ I will ride and light in gloom.

About Author: Aadil Ghulam Bhat is an author of two books, "100 YEARS OF MY PAINFUL NIGHTS" and "NIGHTS IN SOLITUDE".

Besides english poetry he also has a contribution in urdu poerty and novels too. Although Aadil Gulam associate his emotions with words that make poetry. He choose one of the many different ways to convey his message.

Aadil Ghulam Bhat has persued his bachalor's degree in non-medical at Govt.Degree College Anantnag (J&K).

Being a non-medical student he used to write something in feild of literature. Due course of time apart from his accademic career he start to compose his poetry and finally end up his bit of emotions, feelings and thoughts in form of book.

The poem "ONCE AGAIN OLD MEMORIES REGAIN" is written in escatsy manner and the style of writing is quite impressive over the entire collection of book.

10. WEPT BUCKETS

Once again, a lucent moon.
It's been this way for Millennium.
So here again.
I walk alone.
I'm all alone, i don't know.
And i still walk alone.
Amidst midnight breeze.
I was again sad and alone.
Still i stumbled on my ruinate way.
The fourteenth moon, Cried on its own
No silver lining, so sad!
Jaremaid to cruel clouds.
I saw this scene.
I know I'm lying to myself.
I endure such a fate, felt such a great
On the dark road,
With horror in head, acting happy.
Hiding my pain again.

About Author: Aadil Ghulam Bhat is an author of two books, "100 YEARS OF MY PAINFUL NIGHTS" and "NIGHTS IN SOLITUDE".

Besides english poetry he also has a contribution in urdu poerty and novels too. Although Aadil Gulam associate his emotions with words that make poetry. He choose one of the many different ways to convey his message.

Aadil Ghulam Bhat has persued his bachalor's degree in non-medical at Govt.Degree College Anantnag (J&K). Being a non-medical student he used to write something in feild of literature. Due course of time apart from his accademic career he start to compose his poetry and finally end up his bit of emotions, feelings and thoughts in form of book.

The poem "WEPT BUCKETS" is written in escatsy manner and the style of writing is quite impressive over the entire collection of book.

11. VALE OF SORROWS

I'm afraid of my pale face and vale of tears.

Though! I exclaim veriety with profound grief.

Although! My time was running like a dream in brief.

I'm like a corpse, I have fear inside me.

My own little world turned into a darkling dingle.

I felt myself bosky, like in brume, like in deep.

Nothing besides me, I,m inhume in isle.

I wanna reap my each and every grief.

I've learnt to be patient from silent mountains.

I' ve felt the solitude of a lonely isle.

The quit flow of sea has taught me how to live.

After a long, tonight I'm waiting for my lost partarre.

About Author: Aadil Ghulam Bhat is an author of two books, "100 YEARS OF MY PAINFUL NIGHTS" and

"NIGHTS IN SOLITUDE".

Besides english poetry he also has a contribution in urdu poerty and novels too. Although Aadil Gulam associate his emotions with words that make poetry. He choose one of the many different ways to convey his message.

Aadil Ghulam Bhat has persued his bachalor's degree in non-medical at Govt.Degree College Anantnag (J&K). Being a non-medical student he used to write something in feild of literature. Due course of time apart from his accademic career he start to compose his poetry and finally end up his bit of emotions, feelings and thoughts in form of book.

The poem "VALE OF SORROWS" is written in escatsy manner and the style of writing is quite impressive over the entire collection of book.

I'm sitting at my window with warm blanket, quite ere.
Tired of seeing, I lost, I did not see anything from anywhere in forlorn.
Beheld dark sky at night, i found all stars were stolen.
Look at the inside of the sky, how quiet it is, its silence wreck my pain.

12. HOW I ENDURE MYSELF

I walk alone,
quietly silent like a hog - tie
I start to wonder
Is there even an end .
Where should I go?
Do I even have a verity?
Is there anyone I can even share
Anymore.
I walk alone into the silence as,
Dark night
Wondering where I'm really walking
Where I'm really going.
I talk to shadows
No one besides me
They all gone, they all left
Where did they go?
Sunlight varnishes,
willow branches crimson
I found bulbul, lumber to its nest
Hiding the hurt, hiding the pain.

I found a reason
How to live?
Birds whir and hum
Startles my ferret.
There was a smile
I claim mine
My smile spread like red,
tint ripening tomatoes.

About Author: Aadil Ghulam Bhat is an author of two books, "100 YEARS OF MY PAINFUL NIGHTS" and "NIGHTS IN SOLITUDE".
Besides english poetry he also has a contribution in urdu poerty and novels too. Although Aadil Gulam associate his emotions with words that make poetry. He choose one of the many different ways to convey his message.
Aadil Ghulam Bhat has persued his bachalor's degree in non-medical at Govt.Degree College Anantnag (J&K). Being a non-medical student he used to write something in feild of literature. Due course of time apart from his accademic career he start to compose his poetry and finally end up his bit of emotions, feelings and thoughts in form of

book.

The poem "HOW I ENDURE MYSELF" is written in escatsy manner and the style of writing is quite impressive over the entire collection of book.

13. GLOOMY NIGHTS

Eld thoughts grew in my my gloomy nights.
Lucent moon, twinkling stars arrant me to blithe.
Those cold nights, teasing my sleep, blowing my sleep.
Like on one's own mountain, like demure star.
My heart was drowning like a garden withered moppet in
solitude.
I forgot my hilarity like aves_fox pass the deluded partarre.
Didn't know am i alive , couldn't say my heartless pain.
I lay in bed at night and wonder why i am here.
I remember how did i loose out my happiness.
I was or was the shinning moon, happiness also gone, moon also
faded.
I still remember the day when hilarity used to my treasure.
Nothing remains, i shed my every happiness like leaves.
Despite everything, my pain, tolerence without letting myself cry.
I felt like my heart dies a slow death.

About Author: Aadil Ghulam Bhat is an author of two books, "100 YEARS OF MY PAINFUL NIGHTS" and "NIGHTS IN SOLITUDE".

Besides english poetry he also has a contribution in urdu poerty and novels too. Although Aadil Gulam associate his emotions with words that make poetry. He choose one of the many different ways to convey his message.

Aadil Ghulam Bhat has persued his bachalor's degree in non-medical at Govt.Degree College Anantnag (J&K). Being a non-medical student he used to write something in feild of literature. Due course of time apart from his accademic career he start to compose his poetry and finally end up his bit of emotions, feelings and thoughts in form of book.

The poem "GLOOMY NIGHTS " is written in escatsy manner and the style of writing is quite impressive over the entire collection of book.

14. WAIT IS NOT FOREVER

Every trouble was lending, All the trouble was forever.
I used to live in dreams, sleep to meet my dreams.
What some life has taught, what to learn in some life.
Remembering the past life, Life will be a wish forever.
Remove the filthy life, Took me in a real direction forever.
Her scow have changed, the fate of my life forever.
Have adrift something in life, can never be thought of in dreams.
Yet the odds are diverse when it comes to an end.

About Author: Aadil Ghulam Bhat is an author of two books, "100 YEARS OF MY PAINFUL NIGHTS" and "NIGHTS IN SOLITUDE".

Besides english poetry he also has a contribution in urdu poerty and novels too. Although Aadil Gulam associate his emotions with words that make poetry. He choose one of the many different ways to convey his message.

Aadil Ghulam Bhat has persued his bachalor's degree in non-medical at Govt.Degree College Anantnag (J&K). Being a non-medical student he used to write something in feild of literature. Due course of time apart from his accademic career he start to compose his poetry and finally end up his bit of emotions, feelings and thoughts in form of book.

The poem "WAIT IS NOT FOREVER" is written in escatsy manner and the style of writing is quite impressive over the entire collection of book.

15. TEARS OF OCEAN

World is divided into falseword.
Thy presence in everywhere is coward.
The truth that i can't explain,
And world will not understand pain.
Why will they cry when i die,
I'm homeless bird, I've to fly
Forgot my captivating parterre,
But I'm the broken twig of tree.
Thy laugh, my blood, tribulation,
And all my hoisting in isolation.
All cruel hours like Unsprout buds,
And thy deciet turn my tears into flood

About Author: Aadil Ghulam Bhat is an author of two books, "100 YEARS OF MY PAINFUL NIGHTS" and "NIGHTS IN SOLITUDE".

Besides english poetry he also has a contribution in urdu poerty and novels too. Although Aadil Gulam associate his emotions with words that make poetry. He choose one of the many different ways to convey his message.

Aadil Ghulam Bhat has persued his bachalor's degree in non-medical at Govt.Degree College Anantnag (J&K). Being a non-medical student he used to write something in feild of literature. Due course of time apart from his accademic career he start to compose his poetry and finally end up his bit of emotions, feelings and thoughts in form of book.

The poem "TEARS OF OCEAN" is written in escatsy manner and the style of writing is quite impressive over the entire collection of book.

16. WIND OF CAGE

I'm at my wits end,
And still had a lump in my throat.
I'm going to make an end.
So, Found a kinderd spirit, hoping to float.
Then a moment, even i lost purpose,
As my love freckle with age, nothin adore.
I lift my grief, what could be the purpose,
Fearlessly, i will hold on sight of shore.
In a fix, trying the last burst,
By the river, to find my sailing boat.
And on walls I've claimed with durst,
I'm fed up, not the faint of heart.

About Author: Aadil Ghulam Bhat is an author of two books, "100 YEARS OF MY PAINFUL NIGHTS" and "NIGHTS IN SOLITUDE".

Besides english poetry he also has a contribution in urdu poerty and novels too. Although Aadil Gulam associate his emotions with words that make poetry. He choose one of the many different ways to convey his message.

Aadil Ghulam Bhat has persued his bachalor's degree in non-medical at Govt.Degree College Anantnag (J&K). Being a non-medical student he used to write something in feild of literature. Due course of time apart from his accademic career he start to compose his poetry and finally end up his bit of emotions, feelings and thoughts in form of book.

The poem "WIND OF CAGE" is written in escatsy manner and the style of writing is quite impressive over the entire collection of book.

17. GROWLING NIGHTS

Oh! I am still,
Beholding the winter chill.
Across the panneled walls,
Polished chairs and golden grill.
As of you,
Feeling the breeze and dew.
A silent hope, silent tear,
Tired as pale rider, in brew.
Then a verity,
Covert in reality of austerity,
No dignity in rows of adversity.
So, unaware of belief and reality

About Author: Aadil Ghulam Bhat is an author of two books, "100 YEARS OF MY PAINFUL NIGHTS" and

"NIGHTS IN SOLITUDE".

Besides english poetry he also has a contribution in urdu poerty and novels too. Although Aadil Gulam associate his emotions with words that make poetry. He choose one of the many different ways to convey his message.

Aadil Ghulam Bhat has persued his bachalor's degree in non-medical at Govt.Degree College Anantnag (J&K). Being a non-medical student he used to write something in feild of literature. Due course of time apart from his accademic career he start to compose his poetry and finally end up his bit of emotions, feelings and thoughts in form of book.

The poem "GROWLING NIGHTS" is written in escatsy manner and the style of writing is quite impressive over the entire collection of book.

18. CRY ON MY SHOULDER

I'm of two minds, how to get off odds and ends.
My faith is no longer changed, limits were exceed.
O, my sweet hopes, thou are sugar in mouth,
All hopes will fail, all shadows will fade.
Not taken and loved to beauty of filthy face,
Thy dear steps i used to kiss, in gloomy phase
I may be out of your sight, never out of mind,
And you will find greatest escape, with cry everytime
Every second you would be saudade and remorse,
On this cold, dark and sad night, listening the beat of my heart,
Gosh, "I am missing these days", with painful screams.
You won't cease bawling, will not know what to do.

About Author: Aadil Ghulam Bhat is an author of two
books, "100 YEARS OF MY PAINFUL NIGHTS" and

"NIGHTS IN SOLITUDE".

Besides english poetry he also has a contribution in urdu poerty and novels too. Although Aadil Gulam associate his emotions with words that make poetry. He choose one of the many different ways to convey his message.

Aadil Ghulam Bhat has persued his bachalor's degree in non-medical at Govt.Degree College Anantnag (J&K). Being a non-medical student he used to write something in feild of literature. Due course of time apart from his accademic career he start to compose his poetry and finally end up his bit of emotions, feelings and thoughts in form of book.

The poem "CRY ON MY SHOULDER" is written in escatsy manner and the style of writing is quite impressive over the entire collection of book.

19. THE DARK SIDE OF FEAR

Over the edge of yellow down,
Why you said, you love me?
Not forms any simple hope or lie.
Why you play grisly games.
There's a whisper down the truth,
And always, thy fantasist falls,
On the way to my solitude,
Then i cried a lot sadly, madly and deeply.
Whooping madly in my frightened yard.
They are clouds, brief and duplex.
Am i so weak, No...................?
As flowers and thorns, silent like night.

About Author: Aadil Ghulam Bhat is an author of two books, "100 YEARS OF MY PAINFUL NIGHTS" and

"NIGHTS IN SOLITUDE".

Besides english poetry he also has a contribution in urdu poerty and novels too. Although Aadil Gulam associate his emotions with words that make poetry. He choose one of the many different ways to convey his message.

Aadil Ghulam Bhat has persued his bachalor's degree in non-medical at Govt.Degree College Anantnag (J&K). Being a non-medical student he used to write something in feild of literature. Due course of time apart from his accademic career he start to compose his poetry and finally end up his bit of emotions, feelings and thoughts in form of book.

The poem "THE DARK SIDE OF FEAR" is written in escatsy manner and the style of writing is quite impressive over the entire collection of book.

20. TWO AGES OF MAN

All the life is a game, all the ups and downs are merely players.
And a nightmare in a dark night, surely a truth of life.
Novelty are clouds, tears are rain, Didn't give a chance to thunder.
Flowed in the river of rain, met with ocean of emotions.
In the night chill, all the time i am mewling like a sick kitten.
From the other side orange blush of sun are the kind of comfort.
These are just two ages of life, fear and unfair.
And i saw the taste of venom in the form of honey.
Two ages of mine, passed by aro and smitten.
Somewhere filled with thorns, stones and elsewhere with flowers.
I marched upon the both roads,once in a while happily and sometimes in pain.
And like day and night, they are two aspects of my love.

About Author: Aadil Ghulam Bhat is an author of two books, "100 YEARS OF MY PAINFUL NIGHTS" and "NIGHTS IN SOLITUDE".

Besides english poetry he also has a contribution in urdu poerty and novels too. Although Aadil Gulam associate his emotions with words that make poetry. He choose one of the many different ways to convey his message.

Aadil Ghulam Bhat has persued his bachalor's degree in non-medical at Govt.Degree College Anantnag (J&K). Being a non-medical student he used to write something in feild of literature. Due course of time apart from his accademic career he start to compose his poetry and finally end up his bit of emotions, feelings and thoughts in form of book.

The poem "TWO AGES OF MAN" is written in escatsy manner and the style of writing is quite impressive over the entire collection of book.

21. TO THE ROAD OF REJOICE

To cease my Rejoice, to flare the mingled sun,
To catch the orange rays, to spread the wings,
To unlock the padlock, to heal the inner wounds,
I played many parts, to seek the lesson.
Thou have made me strange, alone and Inconsequence.
I know, if i had a strange smell of my own heart,
To grant me the dragon well, will quench my Thirst.
And thy smell lasts utill i lost my all sense
While painting the sickening walls, bounded to ground,
In my mind and, i thought a slick painted wall,
Like a dream of scared child in terrible night
Then a blurred vision, pale body, red eyes unsound.

About Author: Aadil Ghulam Bhat is an author of two books, "100 YEARS OF MY PAINFUL NIGHTS" and

"NIGHTS IN SOLITUDE".

Besides english poetry he also has a contribution in urdu poerty and novels too. Although Aadil Gulam associate his emotions with words that make poetry. He choose one of the many different ways to convey his message.

Aadil Ghulam Bhat has persued his bachalor's degree in non-medical at Govt.Degree College Anantnag (J&K). Being a non-medical student he used to write something in feild of literature. Due course of time apart from his accademic career he start to compose his poetry and finally end up his bit of emotions, feelings and thoughts in form of book.

The poem "TO THE ROAD OF REJOICE" is written in escatsy manner and the style of writing is quite impressive over the entire collection of book.

22. GALLEY__SLAVE

I'm wingless bird, not to yearn to fly.
Pondering over miseries, long enough a fact.
Weeping blood streams left me so drained.
I'm flowing river, ain't finding end of line.
Oh, what have you done, you wretch,
And in deep darkness i rove.
Nothin in line, sans hope, sans taste.
No man apprise, all hopes are waste.
To a straight road, got nothin for my pain.
Enough to move on, enough to feel again.
Nothing but__ didn't squeeze enough to feel,
Enough to heal, enough to love, live again.

About Author: Aadil Ghulam Bhat is an author of two books, "100 YEARS OF MY PAINFUL NIGHTS" and "NIGHTS IN SOLITUDE".

Besides english poetry he also has a contribution in urdu poerty and novels too. Although Aadil Gulam associate his emotions with words that make poetry. He choose one of the many different ways to convey his message.

Aadil Ghulam Bhat has persued his bachalor's degree in non-medical at Govt.Degree College Anantnag (J&K). Being a non-medical student he used to write something in feild of literature. Due course of time apart from his accademic career he start to compose his poetry and finally end up his bit of emotions, feelings and thoughts in form of book.

The poem "GALLEY SLAVE" is written in escatsy manner and the style of writing is quite impressive over the entire collection of book.

23. SONG OF SOUL

It was morning all shine and rain,
And birds whirls in the morning breeze.
Half awake, feeling the Patter of rain,
With which nature tied me tightly.
That I was born on the basis of humiliation.
Has sign of seal of death on face? likely.
Over the sky, clouds are the white blanket,
A great deal of life, waiting for the crimson.
And soft touch of fingertips to eyestrain,
Feeling the smell of sumbal, and Psithurism.
Crawling like a baby around my bed,
What did i lost, morning blithe or truce of dotage.
Cup of tea(nunchai) held along with butter,
Across the window side wearing cloak worn.
Reminisce with fixation on puddles, petrichor.
Nevertheless, hoping to cease my painful odium.

About Author: Aadil Ghulam Bhat is an author of two books, "100 YEARS OF MY PAINFUL NIGHTS" and "NIGHTS IN SOLITUDE".

Besides english poetry he also has a contribution in urdu poerty and novels too. Although Aadil Gulam associate his emotions with words that make poetry. He choose one of the many different ways to convey his message.

Aadil Ghulam Bhat has persued his bachalor's degree in non-medical at Govt.Degree College Anantnag (J&K). Being a non-medical student he used to write something in feild of literature. Due course of time apart from his accademic career he start to compose his poetry and finally end up his bit of emotions, feelings and thoughts in form of book.

The poem "SONG OF SOUL" is written in escatsy manner and the style of writing is quite impressive over the entire collection of book.

24. UNTOLD WISHES IN COLD NIGHTS

Long ago, morning breeze,
In winter chill,
I'm feeling still,
And imprisoned with memories.
All alone at midnight,
Yet I'm still strange.
So what if i change,
You'll cry all night.
In the wings of silence.
My spirit..... Alone.
Along with pebbles of stone.
No rabble, no clamour in presence.

About Author: Aadil Ghulam Bhat is an author of two books, "100 YEARS OF MY PAINFUL NIGHTS" and

"NIGHTS IN SOLITUDE".

Besides english poetry he also has a contribution in urdu poerty and novels too. Although Aadil Gulam associate his emotions with words that make poetry. He choose one of the many different ways to convey his message.

Aadil Ghulam Bhat has persued his bachalor's degree in non-medical at Govt.Degree College Anantnag (J&K). Being a non-medical student he used to write something in feild of literature. Due course of time apart from his accademic career he start to compose his poetry and finally end up his bit of emotions, feelings and thoughts in form of book.

The poem "UNTOLD WISHES IN COLD NIGHTS" is written in escatsy manner and the style of writing is quite impressive over the entire collection of book.

25. MORNING WITH MOURNFUL CRY

Amidest morning breeze,

with deep sleep,

So calm, so deep.

The birds twittering with ease.

Although, fresh smell of dew drops,

Then i am feeling,

Still teasing, screaming,

Feeling nervous, tired like corpse.

Creeping to downstairs, out of bed.

Looking to morning hue,

Something is due,

Painful night turned eyes red.

While looking towards trees,

Pleasure of dancing leaves,

That i never believe

Then I went to appease.

About Author: Aadil Ghulam Bhat is an author of two books, "100 YEARS OF MY PAINFUL NIGHTS" and "NIGHTS IN SOLITUDE".

Besides english poetry he also has a contribution in urdu poerty and novels too. Although Aadil Gulam associate his emotions with words that make poetry. He choose one of the many different ways to convey his message.

Aadil Ghulam Bhat has persued his bachalor's degree in non-medical at Govt.Degree College Anantnag (J&K). Being a non-medical student he used to write something in feild of literature. Due course of time apart from his accademic career he start to compose his poetry and finally end up his bit of emotions, feelings and thoughts in form of book.

The poem "MORNING WITH MOURUNFUL CRY" is written in escatsy manner and the style of writing is quite impressive over the entire collection of book.

26. FALL ON DEAF EARS

Your cold_shoulder is a scary night.
Why did have fake promises.
Whom you have to love , hate him, merely is your devicen.
No shore in the ocean, i am waiting when the edge will come.
In the grip of waves of grief, out of love, why you left me alone.
Why so cozen? I am pahetic of twig.
Was not adopted, tale had been active every night.
I shouldn't have to feel the colours of love.
Why so deceit? Every night used to call me, "O swallow swallow
little swallow"
I am feeling my life as autumn, my cruel hours are abscission.
Why so ruthless? Every night i feel grief and cruel screams.
Why so birse? Now you look at the verge of misery, hatred and
anger.
And i sway in the breeze, so painfully, i flow through trees.

About Author: Aadil Ghulam Bhat is an author of two books, "100 YEARS OF MY PAINFUL NIGHTS" and "NIGHTS IN SOLITUDE".

Besides english poetry he also has a contribution in urdu poerty and novels too. Although Aadil Gulam associate his emotions with words that make poetry. He choose one of the many different ways to convey his message.

Aadil Ghulam Bhat has persued his bachalor's degree in non-medical at Govt.Degree College Anantnag (J&K). Being a non-medical student he used to write something in feild of literature. Due course of time apart from his accademic career he start to compose his poetry and finally end up his bit of emotions, feelings and thoughts in form of book.

The poem "FALL ON DEAF EARS" is written in escatsy manner and the style of writing is quite impressive over the entire collection of book.

27. FOREVER

Every trouble was lending, All the trouble was forever.
I used to live in dreams, sleep to meet my dreams.
What some life has taught, what to learn in some life.
Remembering the past life, Life will be a wish forever.
Remove the filthy life, Took me in a real direction forever.
People's lives have changed, the fate of people forever.
Have achieved something in life, can never be thought of in
dreams.
It was forever, forever is going to be and will be forever.

About Author: Aadil Ghulam Bhat is an author of two books, "100 YEARS OF MY PAINFUL NIGHTS" and "NIGHTS IN SOLITUDE".

Besides english poetry he also has a contribution in urdu poerty and novels too. Although Aadil Gulam associate his emotions with words that make poetry. He choose one of the many different ways to convey his message.

Aadil Ghulam Bhat has persued his bachalor's degree in non-medical at Govt.Degree College Anantnag (J&K). Being a non-medical student he used to write something in feild of literature. Due course of time apart from his accademic career he start to compose his poetry and finally end up his bit of emotions, feelings and thoughts in form of book.

The poem "FOREVER" is written in escatsy manner and the style of writing is quite impressive over the entire collection of book.

28. WHY TO CHANGE

Everyone has their own world but the world is the same.

Everyone wants their own world but the world is the same.

Everyone runs the world in their own way, but the world is the same.

Everyone wants to change the world by their own way, but the world is the same.

If the world is the same then why people living in the world do not live the same.

Do not change the world to change yourself, because the world is the same.

Change your mind before the world changes, we have to live in one frame.

Look at the world with one glance, then the world will surely change.

About Author: Aadil Ghulam Bhat is an author of two books, "100 YEARS OF MY PAINFUL NIGHTS" and

"NIGHTS IN SOLITUDE".

Besides english poetry he also has a contribution in urdu poerty and novels too. Although Aadil Gulam associate his emotions with words that make poetry. He choose one of the many different ways to convey his message.

Aadil Ghulam Bhat has persued his bachalor's degree in non-medical at Govt.Degree College Anantnag (J&K). Being a non-medical student he used to write something in feild of literature. Due course of time apart from his accademic career he start to compose his poetry and finally end up his bit of emotions, feelings and thoughts in form of book.

The poem "WHY TO CHANGE" is written in escatsy manner and the style of writing is quite impressive over the entire collection of book.

29. THE ARRIVAL OF STRANGER

Like she came to condolence for my sickness.
In so called spooky shadows, while in dark nights.
Then a stranger, trudged the dark rooms,
To patch the squeezed shroud, all and all.
She was magical even with her talks.
Probably a song, that is still echoing in ears.
The power and deep care in her inwardness.
Like a caring mom to new born baby.
I was lying on torn bed, full of bushes.
And i thought, i knew so well
In all of her shrieking, i listen to stranger.
We got so together, breathe so together.

About Author: Aadil Ghulam Bhat is an author of two books, "100 YEARS OF MY PAINFUL NIGHTS" and

"NIGHTS IN SOLITUDE".

Besides english poetry he also has a contribution in urdu poerty and novels too. Although Aadil Gulam associate his emotions with words that make poetry. He choose one of the many different ways to convey his message.

Aadil Ghulam Bhat has persued his bachalor's degree in non-medical at Govt.Degree College Anantnag (J&K). Being a non-medical student he used to write something in feild of literature. Due course of time apart from his accademic career he start to compose his poetry and finally end up his bit of emotions, feelings and thoughts in form of book.

The poem "THE ARRIVAL OF STRANGER" is written in escatsy manner and the style of writing is quite impressive over the entire collection of book.

30. DOLENT; THE WINDOW OF HOSPITAL

In the lap of green clothed bed,
Some screams, some waits to die.
Everyone clings to their loved ones,
With their strange oaths.
Some find their place to sleep,
Sans clothes, sans pillows.
Some wait at doors with tied hands,
And seeking God's mercies.
Tens and hundreds of pale hands,
Still are waving, hoping to live.
without footwares, nobody even cares,
Predisposing in blood banks with fears.
Some with pain, some with fear,
Everyone is like croaking soul.
The rooms with deep and secret disquiet,
Rule someone to birth, someone to death.

About Author: Aadil Ghulam Bhat is an author of two books, "100 YEARS OF MY PAINFUL NIGHTS" and "NIGHTS IN SOLITUDE".

Besides english poetry he also has a contribution in urdu poerty and novels too. Although Aadil Gulam associate his emotions with words that make poetry. He choose one of the many different ways to convey his message.

Aadil Ghulam Bhat has persued his bachalor's degree in non-medical at Govt.Degree College Anantnag (J&K). Being a non-medical student he used to write something in feild of literature. Due course of time apart from his accademic career he start to compose his poetry and finally end up his bit of emotions, feelings and thoughts in form of book.

The poem "DOLENT; THE WINDOW OF HOSPITAL" is written in escatsy manner and the style of writing is quite impressive over the entire collection of book.

31. SEVENTH NIGHT

I've had a nightmare of seventh night.
Time is plodding, still an introvert eschew.
Beneath the tree i , destitute, sluggish and perplexed.
I wonder if I'll remember it tonight.
That flickering bats to enter in open feilds.
To find the old symbols of burned rootsroots.
I've had truly the compliments of moon,
As the flowers of desert in seventh night.
But a grown faith will turn it all,
To blurred memories by the slow deaths.
And miracles of night inhume me isle.
Oh! pity, the nightmare of seventh night.

About Author: Aadil Ghulam Bhat is an author of two books, "100 YEARS OF MY PAINFUL NIGHTS" and "NIGHTS IN SOLITUDE".

Besides english poetry he also has a contribution in urdu poerty and novels too. Although Aadil Gulam associate his emotions with words that make poetry. He choose one of the many different ways to convey his message.

Aadil Ghulam Bhat has persued his bachalor's degree in non-medical at Govt.Degree College Anantnag (J&K). Being a non-medical student he used to write something in feild of literature. Due course of time apart from his accademic career he start to compose his poetry and finally end up his bit of emotions, feelings and thoughts in form of book.

The poem "SEVENTH NIGHT" is written in escatsy manner and the style of writing is quite impressive over the entire collection of book.

32. NIGHTMARISH

Oh! The fear of silence, hammered my sleep.
The darkness grasp me in the soot of fear.
The fear that they place in my wrists.
And let me scream the tyranny cry.
Then the Tyrant blow and growling voice,
And thrumming steps at the mouth of hell.
Even though mouth didn't sound out, but
Was half vision and full hope to escape
I didn't dream the fear of wolves.
The tides of sailing boat along alone.
Noisy shouts scrapes my sleep across the fear,
But the fear was a dream, fear of nightmarish.

About Author: Aadil Ghulam Bhat is an author of two books, "100 YEARS OF MY PAINFUL NIGHTS" and "NIGHTS IN SOLITUDE".

Besides english poetry he also has a contribution in urdu poerty and novels too. Although Aadil Gulam associate his emotions with words that make poetry. He choose one of the many different ways to convey his message.

Aadil Ghulam Bhat has persued his bachalor's degree in non-medical at Govt.Degree College Anantnag (J&K). Being a non-medical student he used to write something in feild of literature. Due course of time apart from his accademic career he start to compose his poetry and finally end up his bit of emotions, feelings and thoughts in form of book.

The poem "NIGHTMARISH" is written in escatsy manner and the style of writing is quite impressive over the entire collection of book.

33. TONIGHT

Tonight, my pale hands witness the volleyed and thundered.
The vale of death into the mouth of hell.
Stormed with deceit, through which i blundered.
Plunged into the false notion of fear and sundered.
Tonight, no reason why, while all night wandered.
Flashed all the rejoice and the glory i made.
On the day in front of them, all the world wondered.
Then the muffled voice, rode and well, shattered and sundered.
Tonight the heart is broken into fragments, truly bothered.
Pain left of me, lost its wayin deserts sand.
Where complaints of heart into heaven of blurred.
Tonight, tonight, i write to defend myself, but unbowed.

About Author: Aadil Ghulam Bhat is an author of two books, "100 YEARS OF MY PAINFUL NIGHTS" and "NIGHTS IN SOLITUDE".

Besides english poetry he also has a contribution in urdu poerty and novels too. Although Aadil Gulam associate his emotions with words that make poetry. He choose one of the many different ways to convey his message.

Aadil Ghulam Bhat has persued his bachalor's degree in non-medical at Govt.Degree College Anantnag (J&K). Being a non-medical student he used to write something in feild of literature. Due course of time apart from his accademic career he start to compose his poetry and finally end up his bit of emotions, feelings and thoughts in form of book.

The poem "TONIGHT" is written in escatsy manner and the style of writing is quite impressive over the entire collection of book.

34. MORNING OF EARLY WINTER

And also, this morning when i woke,
The pleasant colours were turn'd into black n white.
The Apples, still on the trees, shrouded by white.
Still soldered to their branches by frozen snow.
The Paddy grains, in the white feilds,
Hanging to their spikelets,, are wrapped with scarves.

It sems like I've seen through the window,
The near future of middle winter laid over Autumn.
The ending season of harvesting, splash the crops and fruits,
Along the whinny outcry across the watery lands.
It will not stay over long, like a nightmare,
But the early winter snow turned Parterre into grave.

About Author: Aadil Ghulam Bhat is an author of two books, "100 YEARS OF MY PAINFUL NIGHTS" and "NIGHTS IN SOLITUDE".

Besides english poetry he also has a contribution in urdu poerty and novels too. Although Aadil Gulam associate his emotions with words that make poetry. He choose one of the many different ways to convey his message.

Aadil Ghulam Bhat has persued his bachalor's degree in non-medical at Govt.Degree College Anantnag (J&K). Being a non-medical student he used to write something in feild of literature. Due course of time apart from his accademic career he start to compose his poetry and finally end up his bit of emotions, feelings and thoughts in form of book.

The poem "MORNING OF EARLY WINTER" is written in escatsy manner and the style of writing is quite impressive over the entire collection of book.

35. ON THE SHORE

On the coast of the deep oceans.
Moment by moment,where cold tides blow in motion.
And in the middle of a blue mirror.
Even with fear, lived some really happiest creature.
Then a sailor in his sailing boat.
Putting the fishing tackle in their throat.
Even at nights, drawn from their home.
With water, of which they used to roam.
Even God has promised us much mercies.
All heavens ready without pain,full of worthies,
oh! why did we, get into this mess?
If all breathen hearts are equally more and less.

About Author: Aadil Ghulam Bhat is an author of two
books, "100 YEARS OF MY PAINFUL NIGHTS" and
"NIGHTS IN SOLITUDE".

Besides english poetry he also has a contribution in urdu poerty and novels too. Although Aadil Gulam associate his emotions with words that make poetry. He choose one of the many different ways to convey his message.

Aadil Ghulam Bhat has persued his bachalor's degree in non-medical at Govt.Degree College Anantnag (J&K). Being a non-medical student he used to write something in feild of literature. Due course of time apart from his accademic career he start to compose his poetry and finally end up his bit of emotions, feelings and thoughts in form of book.

The poem "ON THE SHORE" is written in escatsy manner and the style of writing is quite impressive over the entire collection of book.

36. FALSE NOTION OF MAN

In the vain, all the world strike the conspiracy.
And sing the song of true manliness and glee.
Sense of justice crossed the distance mendaciously,
All is the reflection of false notion, not to agree.
Although some want a little more to explore, but,
The only fear to crub is, to rise, to fall anymore,
Looser fear to fall and winner drive to rise more.
Of such a wit a man should have anymore
The wealthy, of great ego and fame in his name.
Had a kind of respect, comely and legacy to protect.
Nevertheless, a poor, begger, rich, healthy all in front.
By same oaths, making mere breathed name of god.

About Author: Aadil Ghulam Bhat is an author of two
books, "100 YEARS OF MY PAINFUL NIGHTS" and

"NIGHTS IN SOLITUDE".

Besides english poetry he also has a contribution in urdu poerty and novels too. Although Aadil Gulam associate his emotions with words that make poetry. He choose one of the many different ways to convey his message.

Aadil Ghulam Bhat has persued his bachalor's degree in non-medical at Govt.Degree College Anantnag (J&K). Being a non-medical student he used to write something in feild of literature. Due course of time apart from his accademic career he start to compose his poetry and finally end up his bit of emotions, feelings and thoughts in form of book.

The poem "FALSE NOTION OF MAN" is written in escatsy manner and the style of writing is quite impressive over the entire collection of book.

37. STILL WAITING

Climbing the darkness of sky, and is all dark and bright.
Met with her scow, deep set blue eyes.
So melted in the bonfire.
The smile that won my heart, innocent heart full of love.
The big day was a blue moon, it was a deciet of my sympathy.
Rend, plangent voice of troublous heart, bid me adieu.
Your silent absence is black night, my eyes are looking for day,
crimson and bright.
And i am sorry i couldn't suffer the painful odium again.
Every single day i am dreaming with waking eyes.
Blurred is the life, to not know what is next.
Burmese in understanding, prudence even in sympathy,
Shall be telling very sigh.
I remember the moments, you used to approach me
I hide in clouds like moon, still hiding, still waiting and
waiting.

About Author: Aadil Ghulam Bhat is an author of two books, "100 YEARS OF MY PAINFUL NIGHTS" and "NIGHTS IN SOLITUDE".
Besides english poetry he also has a contribution in urdu poerty and novels too. Although Aadil Gulam associate his emotions with words that make poetry. He choose one of the many different ways to convey his message.
Aadil Ghulam Bhat has persued his bachalor's degree in non-medical at Govt.Degree College Anantnag (J&K). Being a non-medical student he used to write something in feild of literature. Due course of time apart from his accademic career he start to compose his poetry and finally end up his bit of emotions, feelings and thoughts in form of book.
The poem "STILL WAITING" is written in escatsy manner and the style of writing is quite impressive over the entire collection of book.

38. RING OF LOVE

Parterre I cover with blossoms for you,
Come, my star of wars!
Come, let me inhale fresh fragrance of you,
Never dull these glowing bars!
My eyes have fill by the oceans for you,
Deeply my heart is in marrow deep,
Though, no response has nodded me from you,
Garlands of star wars I keep.
What if seeds of love i sow in line?
Forgot resentment, i swear by you
When, O love will you be mine?
Loose out my hate from you.

About Author: Aadil Ghulam Bhat is an author of two books, "100 YEARS OF MY PAINFUL NIGHTS" and "NIGHTS IN SOLITUDE".

Besides english poetry he also has a contribution in urdu poerty and novels too. Although Aadil Gulam associate his emotions with words that make poetry. He choose one of the many different ways to convey his message.

Aadil Ghulam Bhat has persued his bachalor's degree in non-medical at Govt.Degree College Anantnag (J&K). Being a non-medical student he used to write something in feild of literature. Due course of time apart from his accademic career he start to compose his poetry and finally end up his bit of emotions, feelings and thoughts in form of book.

The poem "RING OF LOVE" is written in escatsy manner and the style of writing is quite impressive over the entire collection of book.

39. GRISLY GAME OF LOVE

I the impassionate to play the game of love.
Will seek the spirit of love, blessedness thereof.
Was anguish to love, i the quite imperfect,
But upon whom i fall, i know not.
I've searched for you on every night.
I've called out for you in every dream.
Blameless in due time, but in silent grave.
And my nights are slow, sad and strange.
When my words fall heavily, none come to listen.
No longer need you to hide too well
I the falling leaf of autmn, seek the perfect race.
I the eld thought, seal the deal to heal.

About Author: Aadil Ghulam Bhat is an author of two
books, "100 YEARS OF MY PAINFUL NIGHTS" and

"NIGHTS IN SOLITUDE".
Besides english poetry he also has a contribution in urdu poerty and novels too. Although Aadil Gulam associate his emotions with words that make poetry. He choose one of the many different ways to convey his message.
Aadil Ghulam Bhat has persued his bachalor's degree in non-medical at Govt.Degree College Anantnag (J&K). Being a non-medical student he used to write something in feild of literature. Due course of time apart from his accademic career he start to compose his poetry and finally end up his bit of emotions, feelings and thoughts in form of book.
The poem "GRISLY GAME OF LOVE" is written in escatsy manner and the style of writing is quite impressive over the entire collection of book.

40. OCEAN OF 11 WAVES

Peregrine in the midst, glide down to crimson west.

Awesome standing against sky, promising hundred births of best.

And into the blue blood battle of deep and moving waves.

Then served eleven waves till to made them slaves.

None out of eleven shouting, haunted waves are at rest.

Ignobly, all the eleven can't refuse even with utmost request.

Still singing one more time, forgot about my potion.

And is a glory in strange storming winds over ocean.

No sailing boat, no sight of shore anymore.

Sans tranquility, ocean of eleven waves was not lonely before.

About Author: Aadil Ghulam Bhat is an author of two books, "100 YEARS OF MY PAINFUL NIGHTS" and "NIGHTS IN SOLITUDE".

Besides english poetry he also has a contribution in urdu poerty and novels too. Although Aadil Gulam associate his emotions with words that make poetry. He choose one of the many different ways to convey his message.

Aadil Ghulam Bhat has persued his bachalor's degree in non-medical at Govt.Degree College Anantnag (J&K). Being a non-medical student he used to write something in feild of literature. Due course of time apart from his accademic career he start to compose his poetry and finally end up his bit of emotions, feelings and thoughts in form of book.

The poem "OCEAN OF 11 WAVES" is written in escatsy manner and the style of writing is quite impressive over the entire collection of book.

41. INTRANSIGENCE

Amidst the days of joyful mirth,
When thrown my presence to the earth
Among the gentle thoughts that arise.
Evoked bright tears of joy and love in my eyes.
And your voice was left behind ,
To tell, between the magical wind,
How many times you smiled and stood !
Even all that was majorly good.
The day you brought an actual sunrise, when
Your glowing words in loving accent held then,
Happiness lined up in my slipstream,
In a single cap of nights, so rarest dream.

About Author: Aadil Ghulam Bhat is an author of two books, "100 YEARS OF MY PAINFUL NIGHTS" and "NIGHTS IN SOLITUDE".

Besides english poetry he also has a contribution in urdu poerty and novels too. Although Aadil Gulam associate his emotions with words that make poetry. He choose one of the many different ways to convey his message.

Aadil Ghulam Bhat has persued his bachalor's degree in non-medical at Govt.Degree College Anantnag (J&K). Being a non-medical student he used to write something in feild of literature. Due course of time apart from his accademic career he start to compose his poetry and finally end up his bit of emotions, feelings and thoughts in form of book.

The poem "INTRANSIGENCE" is written in escatsy manner and the style of writing is quite impressive over the entire collection of book.

42. SILENCE

The low winds moan, the true silence is.
The silence of falling salvation is this.
There is silence of striking antique palace,
Silence to echoes of filthy and malice.
like a passing night among the gazing stars,
The extreme silence after the death in wars.
The grave of cadaver leaving after burial,
Is the silence, all silence as dark night.
Profound secrets, fuss back again toward first silence.
From open skies, who speaks to us.
Truth is replaced by silence, the silence became lie.
Silence, silence, silence, became soul to salvation.

About Author: Aadil Ghulam Bhat is an author of two books, "100 YEARS OF MY PAINFUL NIGHTS" and "NIGHTS IN SOLITUDE".

Besides english poetry he also has a contribution in urdu poerty and novels too. Although Aadil Gulam associate his emotions with words that make poetry. He choose one of the many different ways to convey his message.

Aadil Ghulam Bhat has persued his bachalor's degree in non-medical at Govt.Degree College Anantnag (J&K). Being a non-medical student he used to write something in feild of literature. Due course of time apart from his accademic career he start to compose his poetry and finally end up his bit of emotions, feelings and thoughts in form of book.

The poem "SILENCE" is written in escatsy manner and the style of writing is quite impressive over the entire collection of book.

43. VENDOR OF SMALL HAPPINESS

Blithely with an approbation, blessed with inclination,
Where there were merchants of elation.
when they walked together, wisphered with soft words,
They saw a strange vendor of small happiness.
Awakes, unwinds, elaborately reluctant, affable and hard to
know.
There was a little lightning in their eyes, mouth and brow.
The merchants went to the door of vendor at eve,
And they spoke the vendor for all the burden.
Till they lose all measure of pace, fixity in their joys,
I was the vendor of small happiness, felt a spirit kindred to my
own.

About Author: Aadil Ghulam Bhat is an author of two
books, "100 YEARS OF MY PAINFUL NIGHTS" and

"NIGHTS IN SOLITUDE".

Besides english poetry he also has a contribution in urdu poerty and novels too. Although Aadil Gulam associate his emotions with words that make poetry. He choose one of the many different ways to convey his message.

Aadil Ghulam Bhat has persued his bachalor's degree in non-medical at Govt.Degree College Anantnag (J&K). Being a non-medical student he used to write something in feild of literature. Due course of time apart from his accademic career he start to compose his poetry and finally end up his bit of emotions, feelings and thoughts in form of book.

The poem "VENDOR OF SMALL HAPPINESS" is written in escatsy manner and the style of writing is quite impressive over the entire collection of book.

44. SALVATION

let the soul be convention, of kindred spirit
Be humble to mind, not of heart.
Choose the path leading to salvation of dictator.
Of the day it will ruin the existence.
Agreeing the voice of selfish heart will,
Drag to the path full of blasphemy.
Two paths crossed into the salvation
Right taken by mind, left taken by heart.
May be, heart will rein the ignoble gesture
The mind always has a plan to play the game,
To understand, to know, to be a very kind.
Having the control over mind over heart will,
Lead the path to salvation, to salvate the soul.
And the salvated soul is the key of existence.

About Author: Aadil Ghulam Bhat is an author of two
books, "100 YEARS OF MY PAINFUL NIGHTS" and

"NIGHTS IN SOLITUDE".

Besides english poetry he also has a contribution in urdu poerty and novels too. Although Aadil Gulam associate his emotions with words that make poetry. He choose one of the many different ways to convey his message.

Aadil Ghulam Bhat has persued his bachalor's degree in non-medical at Govt.Degree College Anantnag (J&K). Being a non-medical student he used to write something in feild of literature. Due course of time apart from his accademic career he start to compose his poetry and finally end up his bit of emotions, feelings and thoughts in form of book.

The poem "SALVATION" is written in escatsy manner and the style of writing is quite impressive over the entire collection of book.

45. BLASPHEMY OF HEART

In vales, i have lost my truce.
When will you come?
I cry, while you are still duce.
I the solemn and numb!
O, where is now the love light.
I'm waiting still.
The loving accent of the night,
The golden breathes that fill,
The desperation of your meet.
The eyes i want to adorn,
My love, thou are sweet.
Why i seem to be torn
Tears, for your sake.
Relieve me with fragrant kiss.
How could i block the lake
Hold me and turn into bliss.

❧❧❧

About Author: Aadil Ghulam Bhat is an author of two books, "100 YEARS OF MY PAINFUL NIGHTS" and "NIGHTS IN SOLITUDE".

Besides english poetry he also has a contribution in urdu poerty and novels too. Although Aadil Gulam associate his emotions with words that make poetry. He choose one of the many different ways to convey his message.

Aadil Ghulam Bhat has persued his bachalor's degree in non-medical at Govt.Degree College Anantnag (J&K). Being a non-medical student he used to write something in feild of literature. Due course of time apart from his accademic career he start to compose his poetry and finally end up his bit of emotions, feelings and thoughts in form of book.

The poem "BLASPHEMY OF HEART" is written in escatsy manner and the style of writing is quite impressive over the entire collection of book.

46. WHERE ARE YOU

Dingle I cover with Roses for you,
Come, my leman of Narcissus!
Come, let me gather fresh Nilofer for you,
How memorable were these hours with hue!
Deeply the heart is asleep, in lap of you!
Mallows have bloomed in the parterre view,
Still, no sunrise has crossed from you,
Garland of flowers I keep.
i sleepless go. Where are you?
What if they bloom only in front of me?
Who has been able to change their destiny?
Come, my leman of jasmine, come !

About Author: Aadil Ghulam Bhat is an author of two books, "100 YEARS OF MY PAINFUL NIGHTS" and "NIGHTS IN SOLITUDE".

Besides english poetry he also has a contribution in urdu poerty and novels too. Although Aadil Gulam associate his emotions with words that make poetry. He choose one of the many different ways to convey his message.

Aadil Ghulam Bhat has persued his bachalor's degree in non-medical at Govt.Degree College Anantnag (J&K). Being a non-medical student he used to write something in feild of literature. Due course of time apart from his accademic career he start to compose his poetry and finally end up his bit of emotions, feelings and thoughts in form of book.

The poem "WHERE ARE YOU" is written in escatsy manner and the style of writing is quite impressive over the entire collection of book.

47. I SLEEPLESS GO

Ashes from my door, i fling!
How can i frost my cling ?
The shower bird surely will bring,
The breeze to soul, curative thing.
Sleepless nights go, trees will sing.
Like the shrieking birds in spring.
And the thoughts of solemn wing.
Will burn painful logs, then wring
Every state of soaring and suffering.
And sleepless stream of broken string.
I have owed an endless longing,
Like the eternal broken arm on a sling.

About Author: Aadil Ghulam Bhat is an author of two books, "100 YEARS OF MY PAINFUL NIGHTS" and "NIGHTS IN SOLITUDE".

Besides english poetry he also has a contribution in urdu poerty and novels too. Although Aadil Gulam associate his emotions with words that make poetry. He choose one of the many different ways to convey his message.

Aadil Ghulam Bhat has persued his bachalor's degree in non-medical at Govt.Degree College Anantnag (J&K). Being a non-medical student he used to write something in feild of literature. Due course of time apart from his accademic career he start to compose his poetry and finally end up his bit of emotions, feelings and thoughts in form of book.

The poem "I SLEEPLESS GO" is written in escatsy manner and the style of writing is quite impressive over the entire collection of book.

48. WALK IN WET WEEKEND

Thy dear steps are in bloom.
Haven't you heard my scream?
In far off woods, lonely I stood !
Worse things i have been endured.
Behold I shine, my ashes fling !
Upon me look ! Chop this string
Come, let us ascend now to mead.
Throbbing beats, haven't you heard.
The dazzling dew on tips of grass,
A swishing sound like of brass,
The singing dove in woods call.
A restless brook appeared for all.
Each evening thy moments recall.
My mind has run astray, all and fall.
If the worst is bound to happen and troll
I neither dubbed nor foozled the soul.

❧❧❧

About Author: Aadil Ghulam Bhat is an autbor of two books, "100 YEARS OF MY PAINFUL NIGHTS" and "NIGHTS IN SOLITUDE".

Besides english poetry he also has a contribution in urdu poerty and novels too. Although Aadil Gulam associate his emotions with words that make poetry. He choose one of the many different ways to convey his message.

Aadil Ghulam Bhat has persued his bachalor's degree in non-medical at Govt.Degree College Anantnag (J&K). Being a non-medical student he used to write something in feild of literature. Due course of time apart from his accademic career he start to compose his poetry and finally end up his bit of emotions, feelings and thoughts in form of book.

The poem "WALK IN WET WEEKEND" is written in escatsy manner and the style of writing is quite impressive over the entire collection of book.

49. WINGLESS BIRD

A wingless bird springs on the back of the wind.
With tied feet clipped wing floats down to ground.
His slow return, silent walk, crawling like a blind.
Skinned into the warm embraces, bursting tiny wound.
With the gridled nights, with eloquent Sorrow,
With a fearful trill, with his soulful cries.
What will be exalted, be enthroned or to be enslaved,
And now he called ofhandedly, " I will still arise".
As slave of a tyrant winds, sings a song to be free.
The caged bird, wingless bird, that's me, that's me.

About Author: Aadil Ghulam Bhat is an author of two books, "100 YEARS OF MY PAINFUL NIGHTS" and "NIGHTS IN SOLITUDE".
Besides english poetry he also has a contribution in urdu poerty and novels too. Although Aadil Gulam associate his emotions with words that make poetry. He choose one of

the many different ways to convey his message.
Aadil Ghulam Bhat has persued his bachalor's degree in
non-medical at Govt.Degree College Anantnag (J&K).
Being a non-medical student he used to write something in
feild of literature. Due course of time apart from his
accademic career he start to compose his poetry and finally
end up his bit of emotions, feelings and thoughts in form of
book.
The poem "WINGLESS BIRD" is written in escatsy
manner and the style of writing is quite impressive over
the entire collection of book.

50. HALF A WORD

Half a breath, half a mirth,
Half a league, to the road of death.
Accusations to the right,
Accusations to the left,
Accusations to the back,
Accusations in front of us,
Keep us in the remorse,
Those regrets from this mortal world.
There is none to make happy,
There is none to glow smile,
There is none to make horse hold
Half a lie, half a truth,
Half a league, to the road of false notion.

About Author: Aadil Ghulam Bhat is an author of two books, "100 YEARS OF MY PAINFUL NIGHTS" and "NIGHTS IN SOLITUDE".

Besides english poetry he also has a contribution in urdu poerty and novels too. Although Aadil Gulam associate his emotions with words that make poetry. He choose one of the many different ways to convey his message.

Aadil Ghulam Bhat has persued his bachalor's degree in non-medical at Govt.Degree College Anantnag (J&K). Being a non-medical student he used to write something in feild of literature. Due course of time apart from his accademic career he start to compose his poetry and finally end up his bit of emotions, feelings and thoughts in form of book.

The poem "HALF A WORD" is written in escatsy manner and the style of writing is quite impressive over the entire collection of book.

51. THE LAST STRAW

Oh! the moments of ghosting.
well, was nothing new.
I could feel the plopped feelings.
Yet, in the hell fire, i let it burn.
The all my volleyed worries,
one by one they disappeared.
My soul, there is a peace of mind,
Flowers, crowned smile and beauteous flies.
Then the special standings,
In the last night of long fast.
Then the intentions of pure attentions,
I could let it go. And let it all go.

About Author: Aadil Ghulam Bhat is an author of two books, "100 YEARS OF MY PAINFUL NIGHTS" and "NIGHTS IN SOLITUDE".

Besides english poetry he also has a contribution in urdu poerty and novels too. Although Aadil Gulam associate his emotions with words that make poetry. He choose one of the many different ways to convey his message.

Aadil Ghulam Bhat has persued his bachalor's degree in non-medical at Govt.Degree College Anantnag (J&K). Being a non-medical student he used to write something in feild of literature. Due course of time apart from his accademic career he start to compose his poetry and finally end up his bit of emotions, feelings and thoughts in form of book.

The poem "THE LAST STRAW" is written in escatsy manner and the style of writing is quite impressive over the entire collection of book.

52. POEM INSIDE ME

There is a poem inside me,
That no paper can handle.
A little bit off all myself.
If i vibe, i vibe. May be
I'm just hard to overlove.
I've infinite imaginary gardens,
Sealed with real toads,
With the intimacy of being understood.
And there is a light of hope,
In wonder, of what kind the softness
Inside me is yet to be being.
Then sometimes, i still pretended
That, it's me, not a poem
Who is still pinning the lights of hope.

About Author: Aadil Ghulam Bhat is an author of two books, "100 YEARS OF MY PAINFUL NIGHTS" and

"NIGHTS IN SOLITUDE".

Besides english poetry he also has a contribution in urdu poerty and novels too. Although Aadil Gulam associate his emotions with words that make poetry. He choose one of the many different ways to convey his message.

Aadil Ghulam Bhat has persued his bachalor's degree in non-medical at Govt.Degree College Anantnag (J&K).

Being a non-medical student he used to write something in feild of literature. Due course of time apart from his accademic career he start to compose his poetry and finally end up his bit of emotions, feelings and thoughts in form of book.

The poem "POEM INSIDE ME" is written in escatsy manner and the style of writing is quite impressive over the entire collection of book.

53. SOLEMN THOUGHT

O, my beloved,
without you, i am haunted.
In your love,
I've felt the soul being taunted.
Although,
Thou are twig, i am still dove.
I learned too late,
All and all, in my heart,
How to love.
I've waited long,
O, my love, come my love,
Overcome my breathless vigilant.

About Author: Aadil Ghulam Bhat is an author of two books, "100 YEARS OF MY PAINFUL NIGHTS" and

"NIGHTS IN SOLITUDE".

Besides english poetry he also has a contribution in urdu poerty and novels too. Although Aadil Gulam associate his emotions with words that make poetry. He choose one of the many different ways to convey his message.

Aadil Ghulam Bhat has persued his bachalor's degree in non-medical at Govt.Degree College Anantnag (J&K). Being a non-medical student he used to write something in feild of literature. Due course of time apart from his accademic career he start to compose his poetry and finally end up his bit of emotions, feelings and thoughts in form of book.

The poem "SOLEMN THOUGHT" is written in escatsy manner and the style of writing is quite impressive over the entire collection of book.

54. RETURN MY YEARS!

I may seek the lonelier way
Where i fill my another day
In the wind of dark fears
I'm soundless, Ay.... return my years.
Yet the mist reposing within me.
And of painful nights to gridled desgtiny.
In the solitude of dark mist, i stood.
Begging to return my lost years from hood.
The day will end now, walk to sky
In the solitude of my souls, i cry.
From the cage of tyranny, all i bears.
i'm upwrought with confusion, so return my years.

About Author: Aadil Ghulam Bhat is an author of two
books, "100 YEARS OF MY PAINFUL NIGHTS" and

"NIGHTS IN SOLITUDE".

Besides english poetry he also has a contribution in urdu poerty and novels too. Although Aadil Gulam associate his emotions with words that make poetry. He choose one of the many different ways to convey his message.

Aadil Ghulam Bhat has persued his bachalor's degree in non-medical at Govt.Degree College Anantnag (J&K). Being a non-medical student he used to write something in feild of literature. Due course of time apart from his accademic career he start to compose his poetry and finally end up his bit of emotions, feelings and thoughts in form of book.

The poem "RETURN MY YEARS" is written in escatsy manner and the style of writing is quite impressive over the entire collection of book.

About Author

Adil ghulam bhat, the poet and the author of a poetry book "100 years of my painful nights", " Nights in solitude ".

Aadil Ghulam always thought that Poetry does not have such tips because it is the art of expressing emotions, feelings and can never be based on tips. Poetry is a profound literature and plays a role with proper system.

His creative writing technique is usually characterized by a certain rhythm and style. As a poet he wore many hats: he wrote Urdu ghazals, produce a fictional genre, create poetry books and wrote a Novel.

Bhat thought he will contribute in literature as much as possible can be done and is just a debut, the whole thing is just yet to come.

Every person has a stockpile of abilities. Then why are still dearth.The only intellect is that we don't let out the secluded implicit and prospect inside us.

#AADIL_GHULAM_BHAT.